Fun Activities For Bible Learning

Creative Teaching Aids
For The Church Classroom

Mary Rose Pearson

CSS Publishing Company, Inc., Lima, Ohio

To Christine Tangvald,
a lovely, vivacious lady
and an outstanding author of children's books.
Thank you for being a helpful encourager to me.

Some scripture quotations are from the *King James Version of the Bible*, in the public domain.

Some scripture quotations are from the Holy Bible, New International Version. Copyright © 1973, 1978, 1984 International Bible Society. Used by permission of Zondervan Bible Publishers. All rights reserved.

ISBN 0-7880-1522-2

Suggestions To Teachers And Parents

Want to add a little more pizzazz to your Bible teaching? Need some variety, change of pace, and fun in your classroom? Here are activities that provide all this while:
- reinforcing a Bible lesson.
- teaching memory work.
- helping children retain valuable information.
- encouraging cooperation or proper interaction with others.
- emphasizing important lessons about kindness, consideration or others, and sharing.

These activities may be used as:
- tools while teaching.
- a follow-up after a lesson for emphasis.
- a break during teaching segments.
- filling time wisely when the lessons are finished.
- something for the "early birds" to do.

Most of these activities may be used in Sunday school, children's church, vacation Bible school, Bible clubs, Christian camps, Christian or home schools, or family Bible-teaching times. Repeat them often. Children like to do familiar things, and the repetition provides them with long-term memory retention.

Parents, while some of the activities require a group of children, many are suitable or can be adapted for use with one or two children. You could even involve the whole family!

The Table Of Contents lists the various activities in their categories, and the Index names general Bible teachings and the activities which can be used with them. The puzzles, activities, and similar materials may be copied for classroom use.

May God bless you in your wonderful work of teaching the Bible to children, and may this book aid you in your efforts.

Psalm 71:17-18

Table Of Contents

I. Puzzles

II. Paper And Pencil Games

III. Memory Work Activities

IV. Bible Drill Games

V. Board Games

VI. Active Games

1. Character And Animal Match-up

Draw a line from each Bible character to an animal which had something to do with him or her. In what way are all these people and animals alike? Find the answer by writing the letter of the animal under the numeral of the character in the boxes.

1. Jonah	A. pairs of animals
2. Eve	D. frogs
3. Balaam	E. donkey
4. Elijah	F. pigs
5. David	H. serpent
6. Rebecca	I. fiery serpents
7. Pharaoh	K. fish with coin in its mouth
8. Israelites	L. ravens
9. Adam	M. lions
10. Daniel	O. sheep
11. Noah	R. camel
12. Peter	S. all animals (he named them)
13. The Prodigal Son	T. big fish

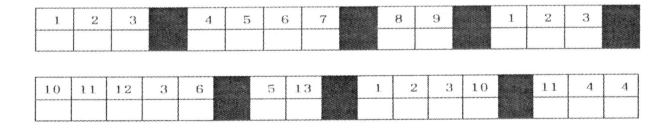

Proverbs 22:2

1. Character And Animal Match-up

Draw a line from each Bible character to an animal which had something to do with him or her. In what way are all these people and animals alike? Find the answer by writing the letter of the animal under the numeral of the character in the boxes.

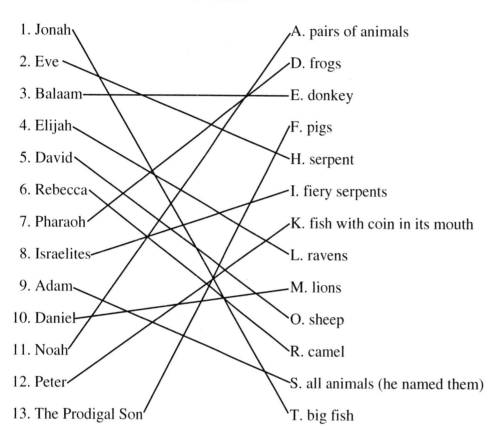

1. Jonah
2. Eve
3. Balaam
4. Elijah
5. David
6. Rebecca
7. Pharaoh
8. Israelites
9. Adam
10. Daniel
11. Noah
12. Peter
13. The Prodigal Son

A. pairs of animals
D. frogs
E. donkey
F. pigs
H. serpent
I. fiery serpents
K. fish with coin in its mouth
L. ravens
M. lions
O. sheep
R. camel
S. all animals (he named them)
T. big fish

1	2	3		4	5	6	7		8	9		1	2	3	
T	H	E		L	O	R	D		I	S		T	H	E	

10	11	12	3	6		5	13		1	2	3	10		11	4	4
M	A	K	E	R		O	F		T	H	E	M		A	L	L

Proverbs 22:2

8

2. Our Special Helpers From God

God takes good care of us. One way He does this is by sending special helpers to guard us from danger. Who are they? Find the answer as you locate the letters in the figures below.

1. In the square, circle, and triangle   ____

2. In the circle only   ____

3. In the triangle only   ____

4. In the circle and triangle   ____

5. In the square only   ____

6. In the triangle and square   ____

God's special helpers who protect us are _____.

Read Psalm 91:11.

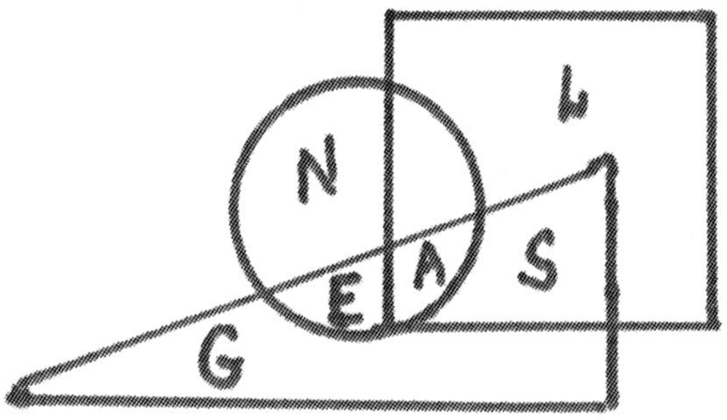

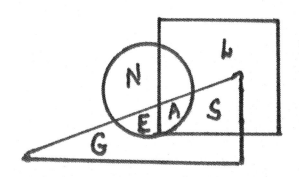

2. Our Special Helpers From God

God takes good care of us. One way He does this is by sending special helpers to guard us from danger. Who are they? Find the answer as you locate the letters in the figures below.

1. In the square, circle, and triangle   <u>A</u>

2. In the circle only   <u>N</u>

3. In the triangle only   <u>G</u>

4. In the circle and triangle   <u>E</u>

5. In the square only   <u>L</u>

6. In the triangle and square   <u>S</u>

God's special helpers who protect us are <u>ANGELS</u>.

Read Psalm 91:11.

3. What Is A Good Friend?

In the list below are some traits which help a person to be a good friend. Print the pairs of letters in the correct blanks to name these traits.

er	ra	in
ov	ri	el
ai	fi	oy
ut	ar	un

l___al   tr___hful   h___pful

k___d   l___ing   gen___ous

f___r   encou___ging   unsel___sh

ca___ng   sh___ing   f___loving

Fill in the missing vowels to complete the following words about a friend from Proverbs 17:17 (NIV):

"A fr__ __nd l__ves at __ll t__m__s."

Do you try to be this kind of friend? Will you ask Jesus to help you be a good friend?

3. What Is A Good Friend?

In the list below are some traits which help a person to be a good friend. Print the pairs of letters in the correct blanks to name these traits.

er	ra	in
ov	ri	el
ai	fi	oy
ut	ar	un

l_oy_al   tr_ut_hful   h_el_pful

k_in_d   l_ov_ing   gen_er_ous

f_ai_r   encou_ra_ging   unsel_fi_sh

ca_ri_ng   sh_ar_ing   f_un_loving

Fill in the missing vowels to complete the following words about a friend from Proverbs 17:17 (NIV):

"A fr_i_e_nd l_o_ves at _a_ll t_i_m_e_s."

Do you try to be this kind of friend? Will you ask Jesus to help you be a good friend?

4. When You're At Church

Read John 4:23-24. What is the main thing God wants you to do in a church service? Fill in the missing letters in the first column and read the rules in the second one. Discuss the rules in class. Can you add some others?

___ aiting for the church service to begin	Be quiet. Ask the Lord to help you truly worship him.
___ ffering is being taken	Give with joy and thank God for all He has given you.
___ eading God's Word	Pay attention to the words. Try to understand them.
___ inging	Think about the Lord and the words of the song.
___ earing the preaching	Listen carefully to learn what God is saying to you.
___ nvitation is given	Search your life. Is there something God wants you to do?
___ raying	Close your eyes. Think about God. Silently pray.

Reading down, what do the supplied letters spell? _____

Do you really worship God at church? What would you like to promise God that you will try to do in church services?

_____

_____

4. When You're At Church

Read John 4:23-24. What is the main thing God wants you to do in a church service? Fill in the missing letters in the first column and read the rules in the second one. Discuss the rules in class. Can you add some others?

Waiting for the church service to begin   Be quiet. Ask the Lord to help you truly worship him.

Offering is being taken   Give with joy and thank God for all He has given you.

Reading God's Word   Pay attention to the words. Try to understand them.

Singing   Think about the Lord and the words of the song.

Hearing the preaching   Listen carefully to learn what God is saying to you.

Invitation is given   Search your life. Is there something God wants you to do?

Praying   Close your eyes. Think about God. Silently pray.

Reading down, what do the supplied letters spell? **WORSHIP**

Do you really worship God at church? What would you like to promise God that you will try to do in church services?

_____

_____

14

5. Follow The Ants To Wisdom

Read Proverbs 6:6 and 30:25. The tiny ants can teach a lazy person something very important. The ants below are going to their nest, picking up seeds as they go. The words on the grains give the meaning of Proverbs 30:25. Mark the trail for the ants by drawing arrows between the words in correct order.

5. Follow The Ants To Wisdom

Read Proverbs 6:6 and 30:25. The tiny ants can teach a lazy person something very important. The ants below are going to their nest, picking up seeds as they go. The words on the grains give the meaning of Proverbs 30:25. Mark the trail for the ants by drawing arrows between the words in correct order.

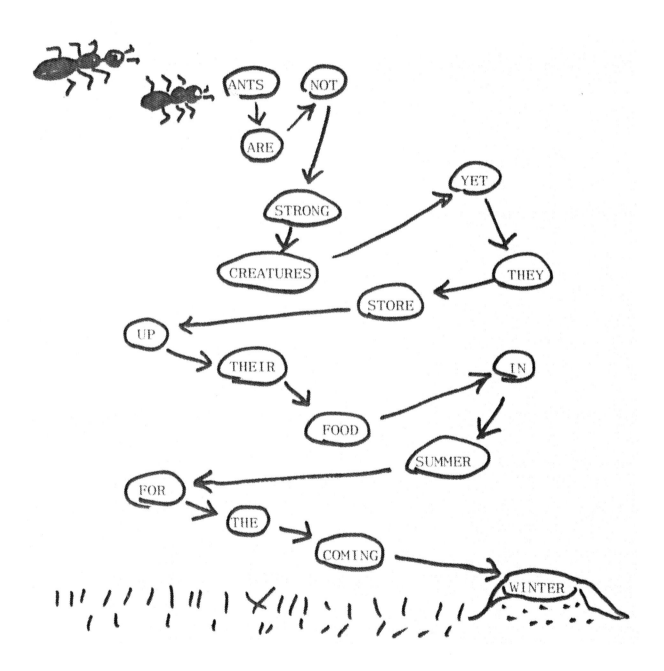

16

6. God's Rainbow Promises

After Noah came out of the ark, what did God put in the sky as a reminder that He would keep His promise of not sending another worldwide flood? A _____. God has given us many promises in the Bible of good things He will do for us. In this poem about God's promises, there are blanks instead of some words. To fill the blanks, add or subtract the number of letters under each line. The first one has been done for you.

A B C D E F G H I J K L M N O P Q R S T U V W X Y Z

God will k __ __ __   His __ __ __ __ __ __ __ __,
       H+3 F-1 F-1 L+4   Q-1 M+5 N+1 J+3 K-2 Q+2 F-1 Q+2

 Right __ __ __ or __ __ and __ __;
      S-5 N+1 Z-3   A+1 V+3   A+1 V+3

He __ __ __ __ __ me a __ __ __ __ __ __ __ __
   H-1 E+4 T+2 C+2 Z-7   O+3 F-1 O-2 F+3 L+2 E-1 F-1 P+2

With His __ __ __ __ __ __ __ in the __ __ __.
     O+3 C-2 E+4 M+1 A+1 R-3 U+2   O+4 J+1 W+2

Copy the words of Philippians 4:19 here:

_____

_____

6. God's Rainbow Promises

After Noah came out of the ark, what did God put in the sky as a reminder that He would keep His promise of not sending another worldwide flood? A __RAINBOW__. God has given us many promises in the Bible of good things He will do for us. In this poem about God's promises, there are blanks instead of some words. To fill the blanks, add or subtract the number of letters under each line. The first one has been done for you.

A B C D E F G H I J K L M N O P Q R S T U V W X Y Z

God will **k e e p** His **p r o m i s e s**,
H+3 F-1 F-1 L+4   Q-1 M+5 N+1 J+3 K-2 Q+2 F-1 Q+2

Right **n o w** or **b y** and **b y**;
S-5 N+1 Z-3   A+1 V+3   A+1 V+3

He **g i v e s** me a **r e m i n d e r**
H-1 E+4 T+2 C+2 Z-7   O+3 F-1 O-2 F+3 L+2 E-1 F-1 P+2

With His **r a i n b o w** in the **s k y**.
O+3 C-2 E+4 M+1 A+1 R-3 U+2   O+4 J+1 W+2

Copy the words of Philippians 4:19 here:

_____

_____

7. How Did Our Earth Get Here?

Many people say that our earth and everything on it came about by accident, perhaps starting with a great explosion in space. Find out what really happened by matching a shape inside the circle with one like it outside the circle. Write each word in its matching shape. Then read Genesis 1:1. Who should know more about how our earth came to be — God, who was present, or men who weren't present?

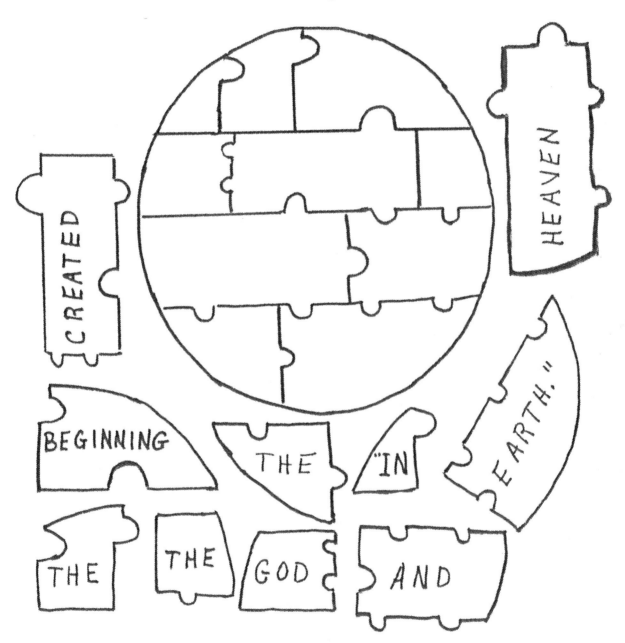

Solution

7. How Did Our Earth Get Here?

Many people say that our earth and everything on it came about by accident, perhaps starting with a great explosion in space. Find out what really happened by matching a shape inside the circle with one like it outside the circle. Write each word in its matching shape. Then read Genesis 1:1. Who should know more about how our earth came to be — God, who was present, or men who weren't present?

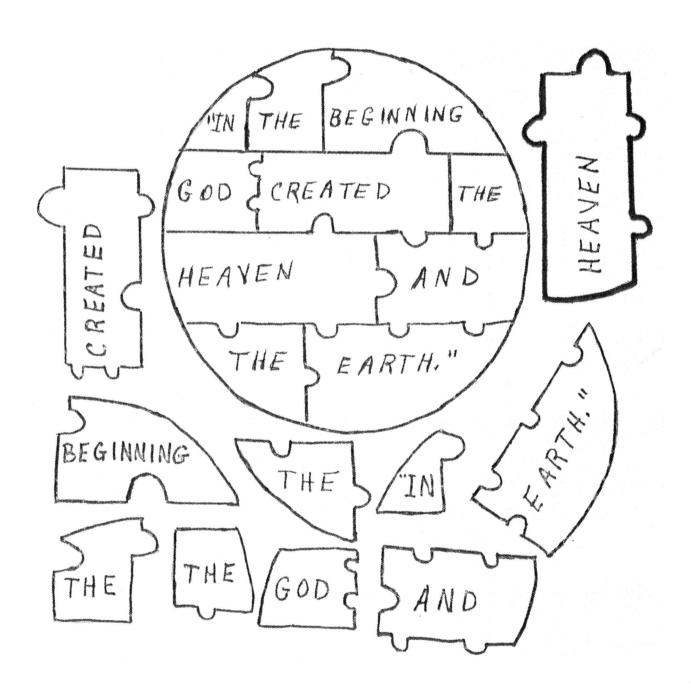

20

8. Remember!

Read Psalm 77:11-15. God wants us to remember how He helped people in Bible times with their problems. This can help us _____ that He will meet our needs, too. Find the word to fill the blank by coloring all the areas that contain letters in the word REMEMBER.

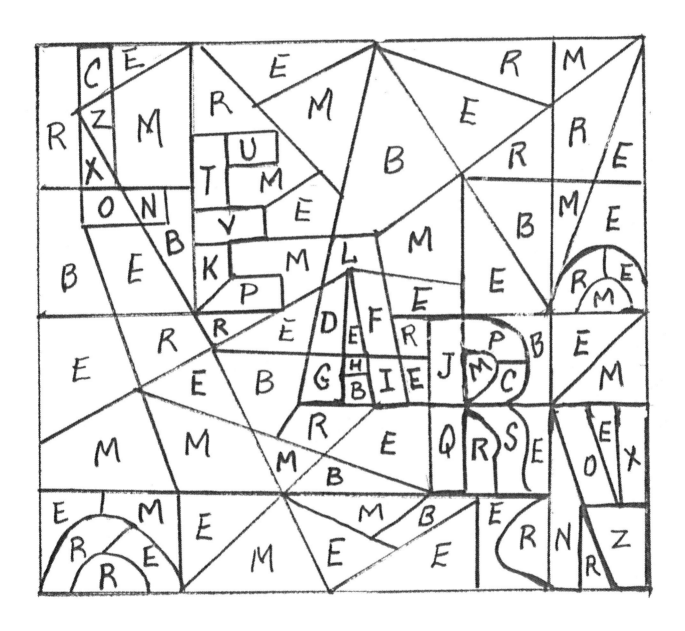

8. Remember!

Read Psalm 77:11-15. God wants us to remember how He helped people in Bible times with their problems. This can help us __LEARN__ that He will meet our needs, too. Find the word to fill the blank by coloring all the areas that contain letters in the word REMEMBER.

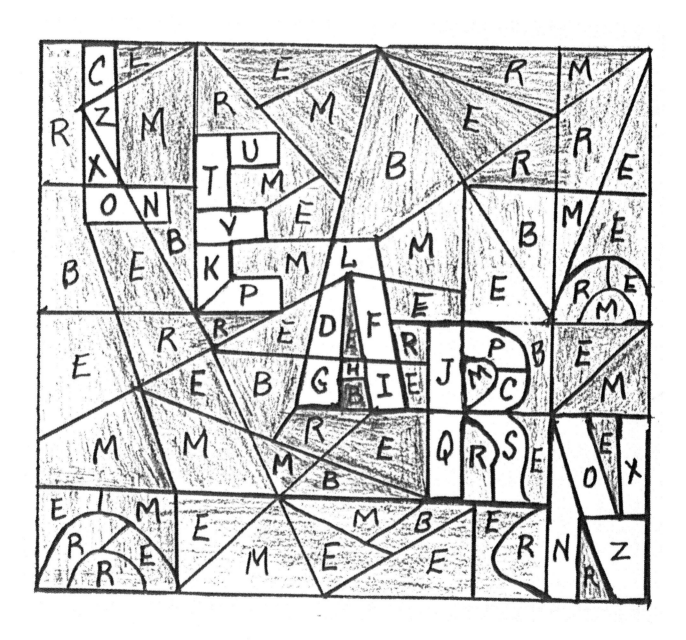

9. Climbing Jacob's Ladder

Jacob dreamed about a ladder that reached from earth to heaven, with angels climbing up and down on it. Read Psalm 91:11. God's angels will help us. We call these special helpers _____ angels. Solve the puzzle by writing the name of each item in the boxes beside it. Then read from top to bottom inside the ladder to find the word to fill the blank.

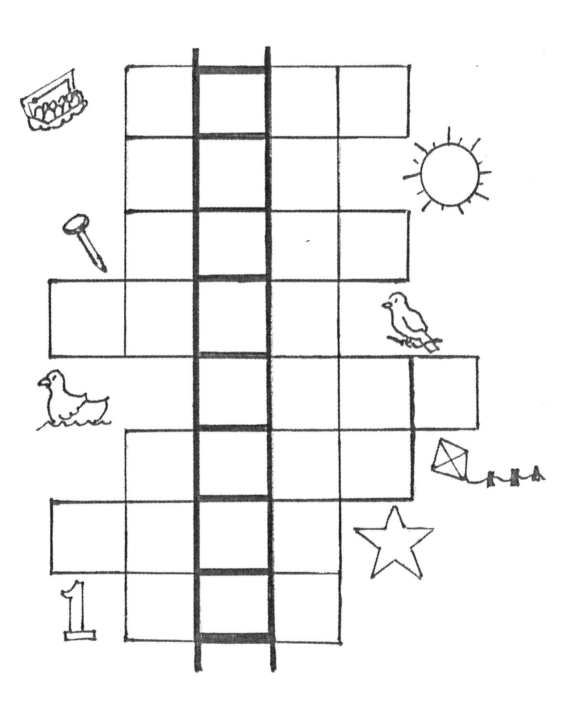

9. Climbing Jacob's Ladder

Jacob dreamed about a ladder that reached from earth to heaven, with angels climbing up and down on it. Read Psalm 91:11. God's angels will help us. We call these special helpers <u>GUARDIAN</u> angels. Solve the puzzle by writing the name of each item in the boxes beside it. Then read from top to bottom inside the ladder to find the word to fill the blank.

10. Brave Bible Heroes

The book of Judges tells about twelve military leaders whom God used to deliver the Israelites from their enemies. What were these leaders called? Find the answer by solving the picture math puzzle. Add to the printed letters (or subtract from them) the letters that make up the names of the objects. Unscramble the remaining letters and place them in the boxes.

10. Brave Bible Heroes

The book of Judges tells about twelve military leaders whom God used to deliver the Israelites from their enemies. What were these leaders called? Find the answer by solving the picture math puzzle. Add to the printed letters (or subtract from them) the letters that make up the names of the objects. Unscramble the remaining letters and place them in the boxes.

J	U	D	G	E	S

(BRIDGE + SHIP - BIRD + E - PIE + DUCK + J + CANE - HEN + E - CAKE - C = GESDUJ)

11. How To Be Happy

If you give Jesus first place in your life, will it mean you can't have any fun and pleasures? Not at all! The way to true happiness is to let Jesus be Lord of your life. Read 1 Peter 3:10-11. Write the rhymed message on the blank lines, going in the opposite order in which it is written. Then print the underlined letters in the remaining blanks. What have you spelled?

3
.you comes all of last And

2   1
.next others and first Jesus Put

:do you what is this Then

?joy real have to want you Do

_____

_____

_____

1. ___

2. ___

3. ___

11. How To Be Happy

If you give Jesus first place in your life, will it mean you can't have any fun and pleasures? Not at all! The way to true happiness is to let Jesus be Lord of your life. Read 1 Peter 3:10-11. Write the rhymed message on the blank lines, going in the opposite order in which it is written. Then print the underlined letters in the remaining blanks. What have you spelled?

₃
.<u>y</u>ou comes all of last And

₂   ₁
.next <u>o</u>thers and first <u>J</u>esus Put

:do you what is this Then

?joy real have to want you Do

Do you want to have real joy?
_____

Then this is what you do:
_____

Put Jesus first and others next.
_____

And last of all comes you.
_____

1. <u>J</u>
2. <u>O</u>
3. <u>Y</u>

12. Can You Name The Bible Characters?

Who are these characters from the Old Testament? Read all the clues. Write the correct name under each picture.

A. _____   B. _____   C. _____

D. _____   E. _____   F. _____

1. Solomon is the king.
2. Moses is holding a rod over the Red Sea.
3. Samson is between Solomon and another man.
4. Daniel is praying by a window.
5. David is not in the same row as Samson.
6. Abraham is next to Samson.

12. Can You Name The Bible Characters?

Who are these characters from the Old Testament? Read all the clues. Write the correct name under each picture.

A. David   B. Moses   C. Daniel

D. Abraham   E. Samson   F. Solomon

1. Solomon is the king.
2. Moses is holding a rod over the Red Sea.
3. Samson is between Solomon and another man.
4. Daniel is praying by a window.
5. David is not in the same row as Samson.
6. Abraham is next to Samson.

30

13. Miracles Maze

A miracle is an event which can't happen by natural law. Only God can perform true miracles. What did Jesus' miracles prove about him? Five words are repeated three times in this maze before reaching the last word of the sentence. The five words are: JESUS' MIRACLES PROVED HE IS. . .

Draw lines from one letter to the next, in correct order, to find the five words. They may go up, down, right, and left. Remember that the final "S" in Jesus' name is the one with the apostrophe. When you have gone through the words three times, what word have you reached? Now read John 5:36.

START

E	J	M	I	C	L	E	S
S	U	S'	R	A	E	V	P
S	E	J	E	H	D	O	R
U	S'	S	I	O	V	E	D
I	M	L	E	R	J	S	H
R	A	C	S	P	E	I	E
O	R	P	L	C	S	U	S'
V	E	S	E	A	R	I	M
	D	H	E	I	S	GOD	

13. Miracles Maze

A miracle is an event which can't happen by natural law. Only God can perform true miracles. What did Jesus' miracles prove about him? Five words are repeated three times in this maze before reaching the last word of the sentence. The five words are: JESUS' MIRACLES PROVED HE IS. . .

Draw lines from one letter to the next, in correct order, to find the five words. They may go up, down, right, and left. Remember that the final "S" in Jesus' name is the one with the apostrophe. When you have gone through the words three times, what word have you reached? Now read John 5:36.

START

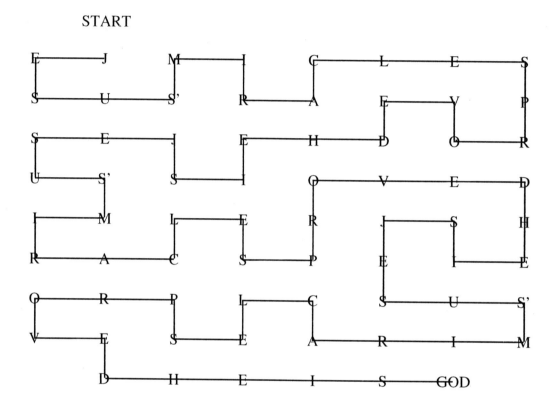

14. What Happened At Nineveh?

God told Jonah to preach at Nineveh, but Jonah didn't want to go. The people in that city were wicked and were Israel's enemies. Maybe Jonah was afraid they would kill him. Jonah got on board a ship and sailed away from Nineveh. A terrible storm came, and a great fish swallowed Jonah. When the fish spit him on to dry ground, Jonah went to Nineveh and preached. What did the people do? Go through the maze to find the answer.

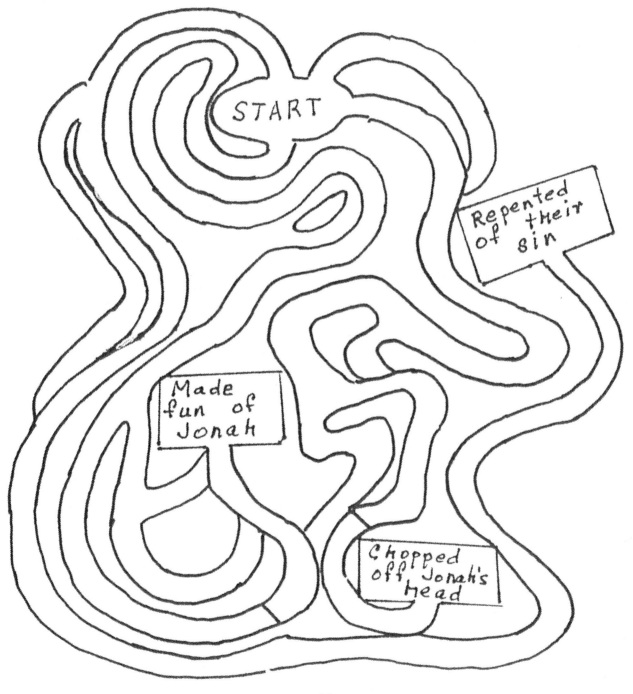

14. What Happened At Nineveh?

God told Jonah to preach at Nineveh, but Jonah didn't want to go. The people in that city were wicked and were Israel's enemies. Maybe Jonah was afraid they would kill him. Jonah got on board a ship and sailed away from Nineveh. A terrible storm came, and a great fish swallowed Jonah. When the fish spit him on to dry ground, Jonah went to Nineveh and preached. What did the people do? Go through the maze to find the answer.

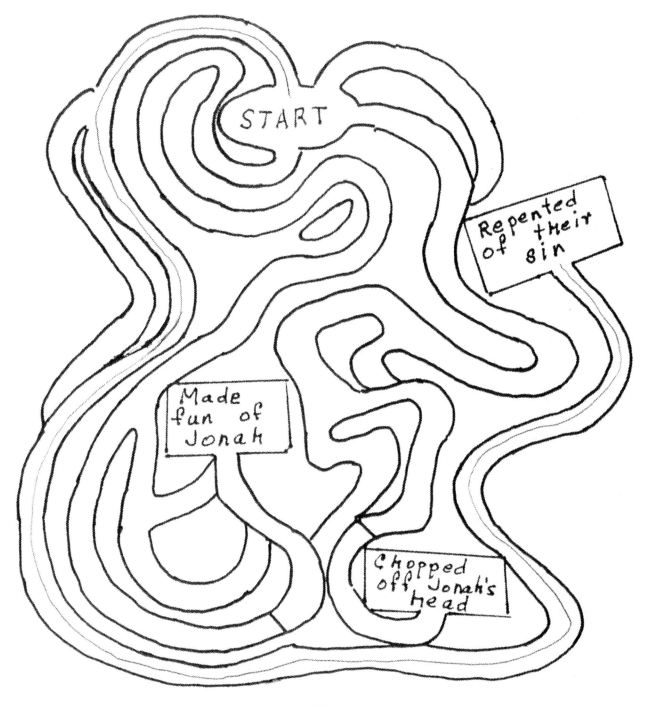

34

15. Peter's Tax Money

Read Matthew 17:24-27. How did Peter get money to pay the temple tax for himself and Jesus? Draw a line through the maze to help the fish find the coin and Peter's baited hook.

15. Peter's Tax Money

Read Matthew 17:24-27. How did Peter get money to pay the temple tax for himself and Jesus? Draw a line through the maze to help the fish find the coin and Peter's baited hook.

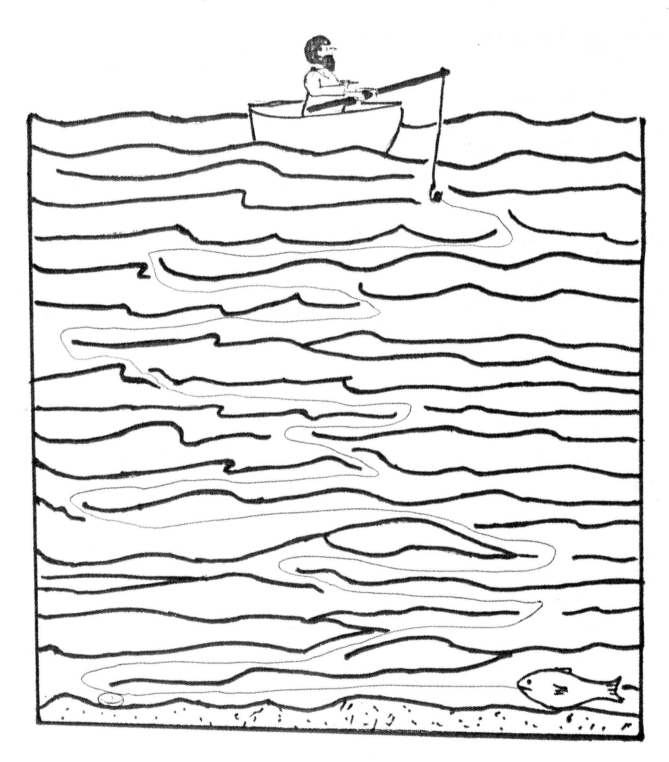

36

1. Which Words Are In The Bible?

Materials Needed

A Bible, a copy of the puzzle, and a pencil for each individual player or group of two or three players

How to Play

1. Play individually or divide into small groups.

2. Some of the words in the squares are found in Bible verses, and some are not. The words which are not in the Bible have references which don't exist. Circle the words which you think are Bible words. If you are not sure, look in the Bible. **(The words in different versions may be slightly different, but you will recognize which are from the Bible.)**

3. Scoring points: Each correct circle — add five points. Each incorrect circle — subtract five points. Add five points to the score of the individual or group which finishes first. Call time after ten minutes or when three players or groups have finished. The player or group with the highest score wins.

"The Lord is my shepherd." Psalm 23:1	"Glory to God in the highest." Luke 2:14	"Eat what's on your plate." Psalm 36:15	"God is our refuge and strength." Psalm 46:1	"Christ died for us." Romans 5:8
"I am the light of the world." John 9:5	"Jesus loves me." Luke 5:40	"Peace I leave with you." John 14:27	"Children, obey your teachers." Acts 12:27	"Remember the Sabbath Day." Exodus 20:8
"Blessed are the meek." Matthew 5:5	"Keep smiling." Mark 15:50	"God so loved the world." John 3:16	"All have sinned." Romans 3:23	"God said, 'Let there be light.' " Genesis 1:3

1. Which Words Are In The Bible?

Materials Needed

A Bible, a copy of the puzzle, and a pencil for each individual player or group of two or three players

How to Play

1. Play individually or divide into small groups.

2. Some of the words in the squares are found in Bible verses, and some are not. The words which are not in the Bible have references which don't exist. Circle the words which you think are Bible words. If you are not sure, look in the Bible. **(The words in different versions may be slightly different, but you will recognize which are from the Bible.)**

3. Scoring points: Each correct circle — add five points. Each incorrect circle — subtract five points. Add five points to the score of the individual or group which finishes first. Call time after ten minutes or when three players or groups have finished. The player or group with the highest score wins.

"The Lord is my shepherd." Psalm 23:1	"Glory to God in the highest." Luke 2:14	"Eat what's on your plate." Psalm 36:15	"God is our refuge and strength." Psalm 46:1	"Christ died for us." Romans 5:8
"I am the light of the world." John 9:5	"Jesus loves me." Luke 5:40	"Peace I leave with you." John 14:27	"Children, obey your teachers." Acts 12:27	"Remember the Sabbath Day." Exodus 20:8
"Blessed are the meek." Matthew 5:5	"Keep smiling." Mark 15:50	"God so loved the world." John 3:16	"All have sinned." Romans 3:23	"God said, 'Let there be light.'" Genesis 1:3

2. Find The Numbers

Materials Needed

A copy of this game and a pencil for each player

How to Play

1. Write a number to answer each question. Find and circle that number below. When you have finished, add up the numbers that are not circled.

2. Your sum should be 100 — a perfect score. If your sum is more than that, subtract from 100 the amount that is above it. If your sum is less than 100, that is your score.

Questions

1. How many ways are there to be saved? _____
2. How many true Gods are there? _____
3. How many days was Christ buried? _____
4. How many tribes were there in Israel? _____
5. How many disciples did Jesus have? _____
6. How many deacons were chosen in the first church? _____
7. How many thieves were crucified with Jesus? _____
8. How many years of famine were there in Egypt? _____
9. How many people were in the ark during the flood? _____
10. How many men were thrown into the fiery furnace? _____
11. How many men did the king see in the fiery furnace? _____
12. How many loaves did Jesus use to feed 5,000 people? _____
13. How many fish did Jesus use to feed 5,000 people? _____
14. How many baskets of food were left at the feeding? _____
15. For how many pieces of silver did Judas sell Jesus? _____
16. How many days was Jonah in the fish? _____
17. How many commandments did God give Moses? _____
18. In how many days did God create the world? _____
19. How many days did God rest after creation? _____
20. How many books in the New Testament? _____
21. How many books in the Old Testament? _____

12	0	4	10	2	3	10	3	15	5
1	6	5	1	7	30	12	7	3	27
1	12	8	30	2	5	20	39	5	10

My score _____

2. Find The Numbers

Materials Needed

A copy of this game and a pencil for each player

How to Play

1. Write a number to answer each question. Find and circle that number below. When you have finished, add up the numbers that are not circled.

2. Your sum should be 100 — a perfect score. If your sum is more than that, subtract from 100 the amount that is above it. If your sum is less than 100, that is your score.

Questions

1. How many ways are there to be saved?	1
2. How many true Gods are there?	1
3. How many days was Christ buried?	3
4. How many tribes were there in Israel?	12
5. How many disciples did Jesus have?	12
6. How many deacons were chosen in the first church?	7
7. How many thieves were crucified with Jesus?	2
8. How many years of famine were there in Egypt?	7
9. How many people were in the ark during the flood?	8
10. How many men were thrown into the fiery furnace?	3
11. How many men did the king see in the fiery furnace?	4
12. How many loaves did Jesus use to feed 5,000 people?	5
13. How many fish did Jesus use to feed 5,000 people?	2
14. How many baskets of food were left at the feeding?	12
15. For how many pieces of silver did Judas sell Jesus?	30
16. How many days was Jonah in the fish?	3
17. How many commandments did God give Moses?	10
18. In how many days did God create the world?	6
19. How many days did God rest after creation?	1
20. How many books in the New Testament?	27
21. How many books in the Old Testament?	39

My score _____

3. Christmas Story Add-A-Word Game

Materials Needed

A copy of the puzzle for every three or four players and a pencil

How to Play

1. Divide the players into small groups and give each group a puzzle and a pencil.

2. At a signal, the first player in a group fits one word into the puzzle and puts a check mark by it in the list. Each player takes his turn, in order, until the puzzle is completed. (Hint: Two words are done for you. Fill in the words which surround them first. Then do the two longest words, and you can proceed easily from there.) The group which finishes first with a correctly-solved puzzle wins.

Words from the Christmas story:

Mary	wise
Joseph	men
Jesus	gifts
manger	Bethlehem
angels	inn
star	shepherds
joy	baby

3. Christmas Story Add-A-Word Game

Materials Needed

A copy of the puzzle for every three or four players and a pencil

How to Play

1. Divide the players into small groups and give each group a puzzle and a pencil.

2. At a signal, the first player in a group fits one word into the puzzle and puts a check mark by it in the list. Each player takes his turn, in order, until the puzzle is completed. (Hint: Two words are done for you. Fill in the words which surround them first. Then do the two longest words, and you can proceed easily from there.) The group which finishes first with a correctly-solved puzzle wins.

Words from the Christmas story:

Mary	wise
Joseph	men
Jesus	gifts
manger	Bethlehem
angels	inn
star	shepherds
joy	baby

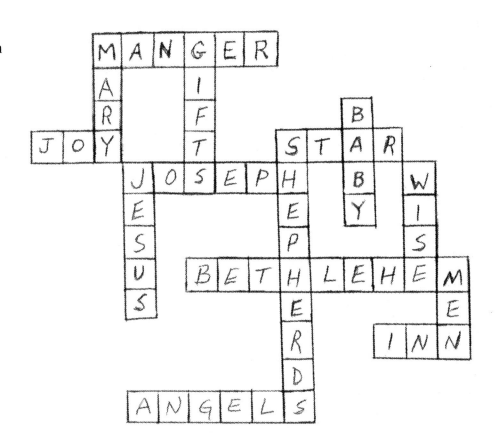

4. Testament Or Character?

Materials Needed

A copy of the game sheet and a pencil for each team of two or three players

How to Play

1. Review the books of the New Testament, which are all contained in the puzzle. While many of the books are named for their author, the puzzle contains names of other Bible characters who did not write a Bible book. Their names are listed above the puzzle.

2. Divide the class into groups of two or three players and give each group a copy of the game sheet and a pencil. Players take turns drawing one vertical or horizontal line to connect two dots. If the line drawn completes a square, that player writes his initials in the square.

3. The player with the most points after all boxes are completed wins. Scoring points: 20 points for a square with the name of a New Testament book; 10 points for a square with the name of a character

Bible characters:

Abel Elijah Caleb Martha Mary Adam Eve Hezekiah

•	•	•	•	•	•
Matthew	Abel	1 Peter	John	Elijah	
•	•	•	•	•	•
1 Thessalonians	Mark	Revelation	Luke	1 Corinthians	
•	•	•	•	•	•
Galatians	Caleb	Romans	2 Timothy	Philippians	
•	•	•	•	•	•
3 John	Acts	Martha	Ephesians	1 John	
•	•	•	•	•	•
2 Corinthians	Mary	Colossians	2 Thessalonians	Philemon	
•	•	•	•	•	•
2 Peter	1 Timothy	Adam	Jude	Titus	
•	•	•	•	•	•
James	Hezekiah	Hebrews	Eve	2 John	
•	•	•	•	•	•

5. Self-Examination: Do You Please Jesus?

Materials Needed

A copy of the puzzle and a pencil for each pupil

Preparation

Before playing, tell the pupils that this is not a contest to see who can win. No one else needs to see their finished paper. The game will help them think about whether their actions please Jesus.

How to Play

1. Read a statement and have the pupils draw the lines as instructed, when they are able to do so. A few of the statements are silly and are added just for fun. There will be no lines drawn for them. The other lines drawn will help the pupils see whom they are pleasing in most of their actions.

Statements

1. If you attended church last Sunday, draw a line from numbers 1 to 2. If you did not, draw lines from numbers 24 to 25.

2. If you prayed at home today, draw a line from numbers 18 to 19 to 20. If you didn't pray, draw a line from numbers 29 to 30.

3. If you read your Bible yesterday, draw a line from numbers 11 to 12 to 13. If you didn't read your Bible, draw a line from numbers 27 to 28.

4. If you have bubble gum in your ears, draw a line from numbers 21 to 22.

5. If you invited someone this week to come to church, draw a line from numbers 15 to 16 to 17. If you did not invite anyone, draw a line from numbers 24 to 26.

6. If you can recite the books of the New Testament, draw a line from numbers 14 to 15.

7. If you have green hair and purple skin, draw a line from numbers 21 to 22.

8. If you obeyed your parents (or other adults with whom you live) yesterday, draw a line from numbers 8 to 9. If you disobeyed, draw a line from numbers 31 to 32.

9. If you have false teeth and a beard, draw a line from numbers 5 to 6.

10. If you helped with the chores at home yesterday, draw a line from numbers 4 to 5. If you did not help with chores, draw a line from numbers 26 to 27.

11. If you memorized a Bible verse last week, draw a line from numbers 20 to 21 to 22. If you did not memorize a verse, draw a line from numbers 30 to 31.

12. If you witnessed to someone about Jesus last week, draw a line from numbers 5 to 6 to 7.

13. If you shared something with someone last week, draw a line from numbers 2 to 3.

14. If you walked on the moon, draw a line from numbers 9 to 10.

15. If you brought your Bible to church, draw a line from numbers 9 to 10 to 11.

16. If you love Jesus, draw a line from numbers 22 to 23. Does anyone know what the two words are? (*Jesus; me.*)

WORD ONE

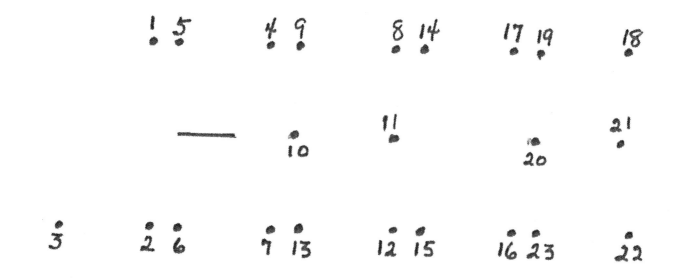

WORD TWO

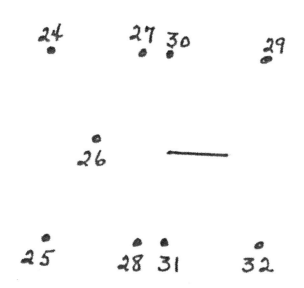

To Discuss

   Look at the lines you have drawn. If you're a Christian, you either please Jesus or yourself with your actions. Did you finish more of the lines on the word "Jesus" or the word "me"? Do the lines show you that you need to do more actions that please Jesus? Do they make you determined to please him — not yourself — always? Do you want to please Jesus in all things? If you do, finish all the lines to complete the word "Jesus."

5. Self-Examination: Do You Please Jesus?

WORD ONE

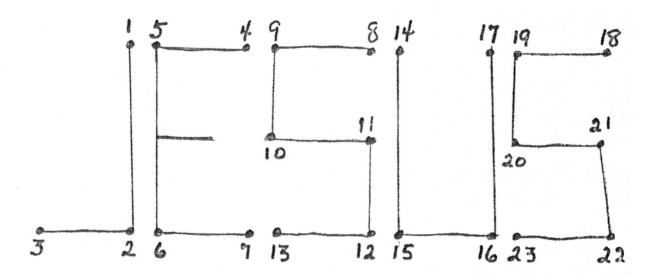

WORD TWO

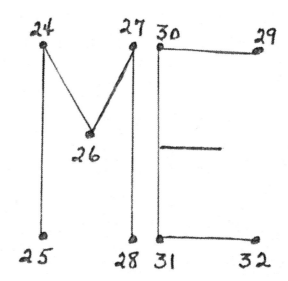

To Discuss

Look at the lines you have drawn. If you're a Christian, you either please Jesus or yourself with your actions. Did you finish more of the lines on the word "Jesus" or the word "me"? Do the lines show you that you need to do more actions that please Jesus? Do they make you determined to please him — not yourself — always? Do you want to please Jesus in all things? If you do, finish all the lines to complete the word "Jesus."

6. Dead Or Alive?

Materials Needed

A copy of this game sheet, and a pencil for each individual or group of two to four players

Preparation

Read John 21:1-14 aloud to the class. Tell them that some people say Jesus did not rise from the dead. After the game is over, we will ask the question, "Was Jesus dead or alive?"

How to Play

1. At a signal, the players read the following story, taken from John 21:1-14, and mark through each word that is incorrect. Then they must write the correct words above the incorrect ones. As soon as they finish, they should call out, "Done!" They may not change their paper after that.

2. Read the story aloud, noting the mistakes and telling what the corrections should be. The players will mark an "X" over any of their work which is not right.

3. Scoring points:
   2 points given for each mistake correctly identified
   2 points given for each correct word inserted
   5 points for the group which finishes first
   1 point off for each "X" mark

Story

Simon Peter and some other disciples decided to go hunting. They fished all night and caught many fish. As day came on, Jesus stood on the shore and called out, "Have you caught any fish?" They answered, "Yes."

Jesus told them to cast their net on the left side of the boat. They did, and they caught no fish.

When Peter knew it was Jesus, he put on his cowboy hat and jumped into the ink. When he and the others reached land, they saw Jesus had built a house and had prepared steak and cake for them to eat. The number of fishes in their net were 103.

This story tells that the disciples saw Jesus. They heard him speak. He put a multitude of fishes in their net by a miraculous act. He built a fire and cooked a meal. Was he dead or alive?

6. Dead Or Alive?

Materials Needed

A copy of this game sheet, and a pencil for each individual or group of two to four players

Preparation

Read John 21:1-14 aloud to the class. Tell them that some people say Jesus did not rise from the dead. After the game is over, we will ask the question, "Was Jesus dead or alive?"

How to Play

1. At a signal, the players read the following story, taken from John 21:1-14, and mark through each word that is incorrect. Then they must write the correct words above the incorrect ones. As soon as they finish, they should call out, "Done!" They may not change their paper after that.

2. Read the story aloud, noting the mistakes and telling what the corrections should be. The players will mark an "X" over any of their work which is not right.

3. Scoring points:

    2 points given for each mistake correctly identified
    2 points given for each correct word inserted
    5 points for the group which finishes first
    1 point off for each "X" mark

Story

Simon Peter and some other disciples decided to go ~~hunting~~ *fishing*. They fished all night and caught ~~many~~ *no* fish. As day came on, Jesus stood on the shore and called out, "Have you caught any fish?" They answered, "~~Yes~~ *No*."

Jesus told them to cast their net on the ~~left~~ *right* side of the boat. They did, and they caught ~~no~~ *many* fish.

When Peter knew it was Jesus, he put on his ~~cowboy hat~~ *outer garment* and jumped into the ~~ink~~ *water*. When he and the others reached land, they saw Jesus had built a ~~house~~ *fire* and had prepared ~~steak~~ *fish* and ~~cake~~ *bread* for them to eat. The number of fishes in their net were ~~103~~ *153*.

This story tells that the disciples saw Jesus. They heard him speak. He put a multitude of fishes in their net by a miraculous act. He built a fire and cooked a meal. Was he dead or alive?

7. Bible Character/Picture Match-up

Materials Needed

A copy of the game sheet and a pencil for each player

How to Play

1. Read each question aloud and have the pupils draw a line from the character's name to the picture which answers that question. (Don't allow anyone to call out the answer!)

2. Players check their answers as you name the character and his/her picture match-up. Who has all correct lines?

Questions

1. What animals did Pharaoh dream about? (Cows)

2. What did Zacchaeus climb up to see Jesus? (Tree)

3. In what strange place did Peter find a coin to pay taxes? (A fish's mouth)

4. At what place did Jacob first meet Rachel? (Well)

5. What three things did Abraham take along for sacrificing Isaac? (Wood, fire, knife)

6. What did God provide for Abraham to sacrifice instead of Isaac? (Ram)

7. What animal spoke to Balaam? (Donkey)

8. On what was Haman killed that he had built for killing someone else? (Gallows)

9. At what place did Daniel pray three times a day? (Window)

10. What did David kill that had a sheep in its mouth? (Lion)

11. What brought food to Elijah during a famine? (Ravens)

12. What did Noah see in the sky which was a sign of a special promise from God? (Rainbow)

13. What poisonous thing bit Paul, yet Paul lived? (Snake)

14. What did Mary break, pouring its expensive contents on Jesus' head and feet? (Jar of perfume)

15. What flew down on Jesus' head when he was baptized? (Dove)

Character/Picture Match-up

Draw a line from the character to the picture which answers the question.

1. Pharaoh

2. Zacchaeus

3. Peter

4. Jacob

5. Abraham

6. Isaac

7. Balaam

8. Haman

9. Daniel

10. David

11. Elijah

12. Noah

13. Paul

14. Mary

15. Jesus

7. Bible Character/Picture Match-up

Draw a line from the character to the picture which answers the question.

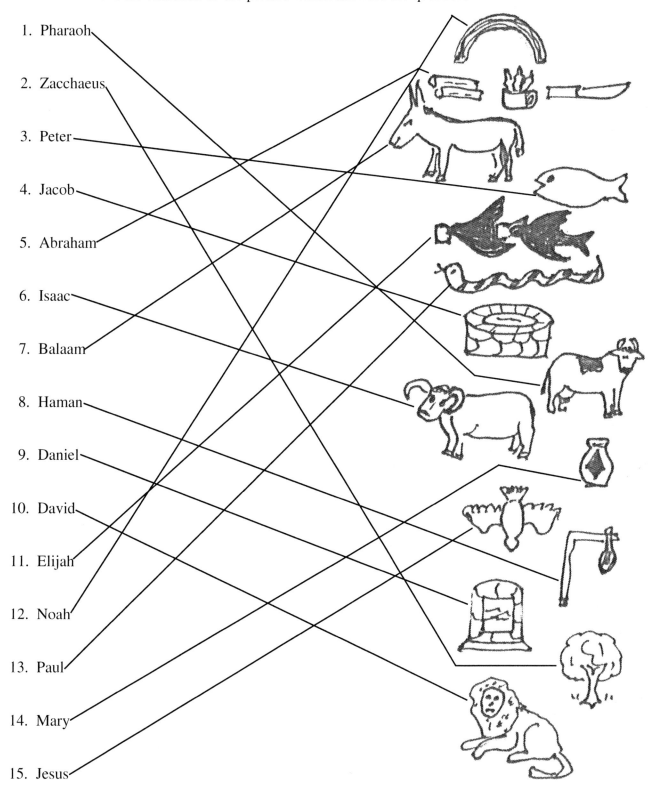

1. Pharaoh

2. Zacchaeus

3. Peter

4. Jacob

5. Abraham

6. Isaac

7. Balaam

8. Haman

9. Daniel

10. David

11. Elijah

12. Noah

13. Paul

14. Mary

15. Jesus

51

1. Find A Word And Line Up

Materials Needed

5x8-inch index cards, red and blue felt markers or crayons

Preparation

You will need twice as many index cards as there are words in your memory verse. On half of the cards, print the words of the verse with a red marker, one word per card. Print one word with a blue marker on each of the remaining cards. Hide the cards in the room before class time.

How to Play

1. Divide the players into two teams. Assign a color and a captain for each team. Choose home bases for the teams, where the captains will stand while the others hunt for cards.

2. Repeat the verse once and announce the number of words in it. At a signal, the players hunt for the cards printed in their color. When a member finds a card, he runs and gives it to his captain and continues to hunt. The captain counts his cards and calls his team home when all have been found.

3. The team members line up, and the captain gives each one a word to hold in front of him, in proper order. The first team to line up correctly with the entire verse wins.

4. To use this game with the names of Bible books, teach a few books at a time. Hide that many and play the game as above.

2. Ten Commandments Relay

Materials Needed

Twenty 5x8-inch index cards or sheets of paper, narrow strips of paper, a felt marker, and transparent tape

Preparation

Tape narrow strips of paper together to make two strips, each as long as the width of your playing table. Tape one strip to each end of the table. Print the numbers 1 to 10 evenly down each strip. Print the abbreviated commandments (below) on two sets of ten cards, one to a card, but do not number them. Shuffle the sets of cards and lay one at each end of the table.

The Ten Commandments (Abbreviated)

1. Have no other gods before me.
2. Do not worship any idols.
3. Do not take the name of your God in vain.
4. Remember the Sabbath day to keep it holy.
5. Honor your father and mother.
6. You shall not murder.
7. You shall not commit adultery.
8. You shall not steal.
9. You shall not bear false witness.
10. You shall not covet.

How to Play

1. Divide into two teams and have team members line up behind each other for a relay, facing the table.

2. At a signal, the first player on each team runs to the table, picks up one card, and places it where it belongs (the first commandment by #1, the second by #2, and so forth). He runs back and tags the next player and goes to the back of the line. Continue, until each team places all ten commandments. At any time during the game, if a player thinks his team's cards are placed in the wrong order, he may rearrange the cards.

3. Scoring: 10 points for finishing first. 5 points taken off of either team's score for each incorrectly placed card. The team with the highest score wins.

3. Little Good Christian Girl

How to Play

1. Teach the names of the fruit of the Spirit, found in Galatians 5:22-23. Here are the lists from the KJV and NIV:

King James Version
love, joy, peace, longsuffering, gentleness, goodness, faith, meekness, temperance

New International Version
love, joy, peace, patience, kindness, goodness, faithfulness, gentleness, self-control

2. Divide the players into small groups. Read the following story. The players listen carefully to see which group can answer a question at the end of the story.

Story

"Come, Little Good Christian Girl," Mother called one day. "I have a basket of the fruit of the Spirit for you to take to Grandmother. There is (*read a list of the fruit*). Watch out for the wolf-in-sheep's-clothing. Don't let him take your fruit."

Little Good Christian Girl took the fruit basket and started down the path to Grandmother's house. Soon she was in the deep, dark forest. She held tightly to her basket. "I must not let the wolf-in-sheep's-clothing get my fruit of the Spirit," she said. "I know every piece. It is (*read the list of fruit*)."

Beside the path, Little Good Christian Girl saw a sheep with white, fluffy wool. "What a pretty sheep you are," she said, patting its head. Suddenly, the sheep opened its mouth, and Little Good Christian Girl saw long, sharp teeth. "I want your fruit," snarled the sheep. "Give it to me!"

"Oh, you're the wolf-in-sheep's-clothing!" cried Little Good Christian Girl. "You can't have my fruit!" But the wolf snapped at the basket, and some of the fruit fell out. Little Good Christian Girl ran away fast, holding her basket tightly, and arrived at Grandmother's house, quite out of breath.

"Grandmother, Grandmother," she called, "the wolf-in-sheep's-clothing got some of my fruit!" Grandmother helped her count the fruit in her basket. There was (*name all but love, joy, and goodness*). Three pieces were missing. What were they? (*See which group can give the answer first.*)

(*Repeat the story, changing the fruit that are missing, until the children know the fruit quite well.*) The wolf-in-sheep's-clothing reminds us of the devil, who tricks us into doing wrong. He tries to keep us from bearing the fruit of the Spirit. (*Discuss some ways he might hinder us from bearing each aspect of the nine-fold fruit of the Holy Spirit.*)

4. Challenge

Purpose

To review any kind of memory work

Materials Needed

Index cards or slips of paper (about 3x5 inches), three small boxes or baskets

Preparation

To review memory verses, print one verse reference and the first two words of the verse on each card. You will need one or more cards per player, so you may have to print the same reference on several cards. To review the names of Bible books, print the name of one division of books (such as Old Testament — Law) and the beginning book of that division (Genesis).

How to Play

1. Divide players into two teams. Place all the memory work cards in a box or basket (the class container). Give each team an empty container to place on either side of it.

2. The first player from Team One draws one card from the class container. He states what it says and completes the verse or names the Bible books.

3. The leader asks, "Does Team Two challenge?" If any Team Two member thinks the player made a mistake, he says, "I challenge." Then he must say the memory work himself. The leader will then state which team member gave the memory work correctly. That one gets to put the card in his team's container. If neither team member was correct, the card goes back into the class container.

4. Next, the first member of Team Two draws a card and repeats the memory work. Continue, alternating teams, until all the cards are gone. The team with the most cards wins.

Alternate Suggestion

For a small class, have only a class container which holds several cards per player. Each individual plays for himself and holds the cards he earns. If a challenger is correct, he takes the card and holds it. Players may have several turns. The winner is the one with the most cards when the game is over.

5. Tic-Tac-Grow

Materials Needed

A posterboard, chalkboard, or overhead projector with a transparency; several 8-1/2x11-inch sheets of paper; two pencils

Preparation

Before class, draw a tic-tac-toe block of nine squares on a posterboard, chalkboard, or transparency. In the squares, print the references for recently-learned memory verses, one to a square. (If you don't have nine memory verses, add some well-known verse references, such as John 3:16.) On several sheets of paper, draw tic-tac-toe blocks with blank squares.

Discussion

Before playing the game, have the class read with you 1 Peter 3:18. Tell them that the key word for this verse is "grow." One important way a Christian can grow is in the knowledge of Jesus Christ. We find this knowledge in the Bible. By reading, studying, and memorizing Bible verses, we can grow in our Christian life. That's why this game of memory-verse review is called "Tic-Tac-Grow."

How to Play

1. Divide the players into two teams and choose a captain for each team. With your hands behind your back, place a coin in one hand. The captains each pick a hand, and the one who finds the coin may play first and choose whether his team uses an "X" or an "O."

2. The first player chooses a verse reference and repeats that verse. If it is correctly said, he writes an "X" or "O" in its square on the class playing sheet. Continue, alternating teams with each play and giving all team members a chance to play.

3. The winning team is the one who completes a row across, down, or diagonally. Play again on a new block of squares as often as you wish.

Sample Tic-Tac-Grow Game

John 3:16	2 Peter 3:18	John 1:12
Genesis 1:1	Matthew 5:16	Psalm 23:1
Numbers 32:23	Acts 1:8	Joshua 1:9

6. Winner!

Materials Needed

Twelve 3x5-inch index cards, a large paper bag

Preparation

Print each letter of the word "winner" on a set of six cards — one letter per card. Print memory verse references on the backs of the cards, one per card. Make a second set of cards just like the first. Shuffle the cards and place them in a large paper bag.

How to Play

1. Divide the players into two teams. Choose captains. The players take turns, alternating teams on each play. A player draws a card from the bag, without looking inside.

2. If the player can correctly say the memory verse called for, his team keeps the card, and the captain lays it on a table, letter side up. If a team gets a letter which is a duplicate of one already there (except for the "N"), that card must be returned to the bag.

3. The winning team is the one who can first spell "winner."

4. Keep the sets of cards to review the memory verses often. Then make up new sets for new verses.

7. Hunting For Hidden Treasures

Materials Needed

Yellow construction paper, a felt pen, scissors, and two boxes

Preparation

Cut 2-inch circles of yellow construction paper, about twice as many as your anticipated class attendance. Mark these "gold coins" with different denominations of five, ten, or twenty dollars. Cover two small boxes with construction paper and label each with the words "treasure chest." Before class time, hide the "gold coins" around the room.

How to Play

1. Read Psalm 119:127 to the class. Explain that God's commands are in the Bible. We should love God's Word more than all the gold in the world. Our minds should be like "treasure chests" in which we store many Bible verses.

2. Divide the players into two teams and designate one treasure chest for each team. Show the players one of the "gold coins" and tell them that there are many more hidden in the room. When you say, "Go," they will hunt for the coins and hold them in their hands, until you say, "Stop."

3. At the end of the hunt, a player must repeat a Bible verse in order to place one of his coins in his team's treasure chest. A player who finds more than one coin must repeat a different verse for each coin.

4. Count the total value of the coins in each treasure chest. The team with the highest score wins.

Another Way to Play This Game

Use this game with the memory verse of the day. Each player will stop hunting when he finds one coin. He must be able to say the day's memory verse without a mistake in order to put his coin in his team's treasure chest.

IV. Bible Drill Games

These games help pupils learn the books of the Bible and their locations and how to find Scripture references.

1. Old Or New?

Materials Needed
Two placards, 66 index cards, masking tape, and a felt marker

Preparation
Print the names of all the Bible books on the cards — one name to a card. Print "Old Testament" on one placard and "New Testament" on the other. On one wall of the room, tape the Old Testament placard in one corner and the New Testament placard in the other corner.

How to Play
1. Line up all the players against the wall which faces the two corners where the placards are. Give each player a card with the name of a Bible book.
2. Say "Go" and then count to 15. The players run to the corner where they think the book on their card belongs. When you reach 15, call "Stop," and the players must stay where they are. Any player who is not in a corner must sit down.
3. Check the cards to see if any players are in the wrong corner. They must sit down. Have the players line up again and give them new cards. Continue until all the cards have been used. The players who are still in the game are the winners.

2. Name That Bible Book

How to Play

1. Line up all the players, side by side. Name any book of the Bible. The first one in line gives the name of the following book. If he is right, he goes to the end of the line. If he is wrong, he must sit down.

2. Continue, naming different books, until all the books have been named. The players who are still standing are the winners. If no player survives through all the books, there are no winners. Play this game often, until many pupils can name the Bible books in order.

Suggestion

If most of your pupils don't know the Bible books in order, teach a few at a time, repeating them over and over. Then call the name of one of those books and see if the class can name the following book. Play the above game with just those books, and then proceed to teach other books.

3. Where Is It?

How to Play

1. Have the players line up side by side. Give the name of a Bible book or some name that is not a Bible book. Then count to five. If the book is in the New Testament, players raise their right hand. If it is in the Old Testament, they raise their left hand. If it is not the name of a Bible book, they hold both hands still, straight down.

2. The players must hold their hands where they are at the count of five. Those whose hands are held correctly stay in the game. Those whose hands are wrong must sit down. Play as long as you wish. Those still standing at the end of the game are the winners.

3. Some suggested names which are not Bible books: Hezekiah, Joseph, Adam, Andrew, Philip, Thomas, Thaddeus, Bartholomew, Caleb, Noah, Moses, Israel, and David.

4. Bible Traveler

Purpose

This game uses the Bible drill, "Travel the Roman Road," in which pupils hunt verses in the book of Romans only. The drill will help them become familiar with important verses about salvation and Christian living. The game may also be used with Bible drills or quiz questions about places where Jesus or other Bible characters traveled in Bible lands.

Materials Needed

A chalkboard and chalk or a posterboard or large piece of paper and a felt marker, a Bible for each pupil

Preparation

Draw lines two inches apart and about one foot long on a chalkboard, posterboard, or large piece of paper. Print the initials of each player, circled, on the starting line (see the drawing).

How to Play

1. Have all players stand in a line, with their closed Bibles on the palm of one hand at waist level, Genesis up, and the other hand on top of the Bible. Conduct the drill, first reading the statement and then calling out the reference. The pupils hold still until you say, "Charge!"

2. Pupils hunt for the verse. When they find it, they step forward one step, with a finger on the reference. When three pupils have stepped out, call, "Stop!" All players stop hunting.

3. The first one who stepped forward reads. If he has a correct verse, place his initials on the first line of the drawing. If he reads the wrong verse, the second one to step out (or the third, if necessary) reads. Continue, even if you must repeat the same references, until one player has reached the goal line.

4. With a large group, divide into two teams. Choose a color for each team. Proceed as above, with a colored circle indicating the line to which the team has progressed.

Bible Traveler Game Chart

7. _____ goal line
6. _____
5. _____
4. _____
3. _____
2. _____
1. _____

(CA) (DE) (WS) (RT) (AF) (BJ) (CN) (OP)

_ starting line

Bible Drill: Travel The Roman Road

1. All have sinned. Romans 3:23

2. Sin pays awful wages. Romans 6:23

3. God loves us and Jesus died for us. Romans 5:8

4. Believe on Jesus and confess him as Lord. Romans 10:9

5. When we believe on Jesus and confess him as Savior and Lord, we are saved. Romans 10:10

6. All people may call on Jesus and be saved. Romans 10:13

7. We have peace with God through faith. Romans 5:1

8. When we believe, we become God's children. Romans 8:16

9. God wants us to give our bodies to Him. Romans 12:1

10. Always glorify God. Romans 15:6

11. Don't be ashamed of Christ or his gospel. Romans 1:16

Repeat this drill often, especially the first six verses, so that your pupils may learn to use them in winning others to Christ. After several such drills, see if the children can find the reference when you give the statement only.

5. Zap Those Flaming Arrows

Materials Needed

A copy of this game, a Bible, and a pencil for each pupil or group of two or three players

Discussion

Everyone should look at Matthew 4:4, 7, and 10. What three words did Jesus repeat after each temptation of the devil? (*It is written.*) Jesus quoted Bible verses with each temptation, didn't he? We can do the same thing. This will help us say no to the temptation. What will we need to do before we can quote the verses? (*Memorize them.*)

How to Play

1. At a signal, each individual or group of players hunts the first verse and then finds the temptation that fits it best. They draw a line from the verse to that temptation. Continue matching verses and temptations until all the lines are drawn. When they have finished, they call out, "Done!"

2. When all have completed the match-up, read the correct matches. Players will put an "X" beside each verse which is matched incorrectly. Deduct ten points for every "X." The first individual or group to finish gets five points. The highest score wins.

Zap The Flaming Arrows Of The Devil

The Bible calls Satan's temptations "flaming arrows." Saying a Bible verse could help you zap his flaming arrows. Read each verse and draw a line from it to the temptation it fits best.

1. Ephesians 6:2	Steal a dollar.
2. Psalm 101:3	Disobey your father.
3. Leviticus 19:18	Tell a lie.
4. Exodus 20:15	Watch an "R"-rated movie
5. Psalm 122:1	Wish to own your friend's bike
6. Matthew 10:8	Drink an alcoholic beverage
7. Ephesians 6:1	Stay away from church.
8. Proverbs 23:31	Talk back to your parents.
9. Exodus 20:17	Keep your money for yourself.
10. Colossians 3:9	Hate a neighbor's child.

5. Zap Those Flaming Arrows

Materials Needed

A copy of this game, a Bible, and a pencil for each pupil or group of two or three players

Discussion

Everyone should look at Matthew 4:4, 7, and 10. What three words did Jesus repeat after each temptation of the devil? (*It is written.*) Jesus quoted Bible verses with each temptation, didn't he? We can do the same thing. This will help us say no to the temptation. What will we need to do before we can quote the verses? (*Memorize them.*)

How to Play

1. At a signal, each individual or group of players hunts the first verse and then finds the temptation that fits it best. They draw a line from the verse to that temptation. Continue matching verses and temptations until all the lines are drawn. When they have finished, they call out, "Done!"

2. When all have completed the match-up, read the correct matches. Players will put an "X" beside each verse which is matched incorrectly. Deduct ten points for every "X." The first individual or group to finish gets five points. The highest score wins.

Zap The Flaming Arrows Of The Devil

The Bible calls Satan's temptations "flaming arrows." Saying a Bible verse could help you zap his flaming arrows. Read each verse and draw a line from it to the temptation it fits best.

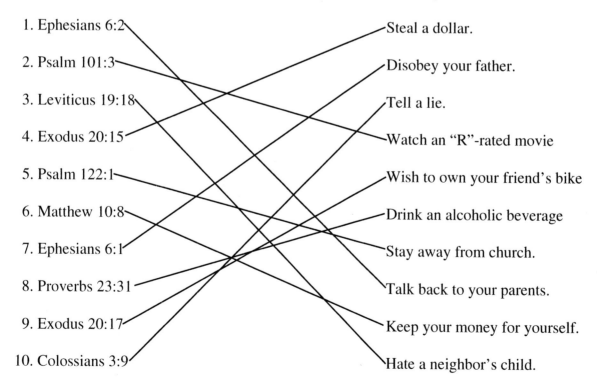

1. Ephesians 6:2   Steal a dollar.

2. Psalm 101:3   Disobey your father.

3. Leviticus 19:18   Tell a lie.

4. Exodus 20:15   Watch an "R"-rated movie

5. Psalm 122:1   Wish to own your friend's bike

6. Matthew 10:8   Drink an alcoholic beverage

7. Ephesians 6:1   Stay away from church.

8. Proverbs 23:31   Talk back to your parents.

9. Exodus 20:17   Keep your money for yourself.

10. Colossians 3:9   Hate a neighbor's child.

6. How To Be Rich

Purpose
To show that earthly riches can't satisfy, but living for Jesus brings satisfaction and joy

Materials Needed
A bag containing sixty pieces of play money or pennies, small paper bags, a Bible for each pupil

Preparation
For a large class, provide one small paper bag for each team. For a small class, have one bag for each player.

How to Play
1. Divide the pupils into two teams and line them up, with their Bibles ready for a Bible drill. Give each team an empty small paper bag. Using the verses about money and riches, conduct the drill. Call time when four players have stepped forward.

2. The first player who steps out reads the verse. If he reads the right one, he may take two pennies or pieces of play money from the money bag and place them in his team's paper bag. The second player who steps forward, if his finger is on the right verse, may put one piece of money in his team's bag.

3. If either of the first two players are wrong, the next player in order may try to earn the money. The team with the most money at the end of the drill is the winner.

4. For a small class, each player should have his own paper bag and receive pieces of money as stated above.

Bible Verses About Money Or Riches

Isaiah 55:1	Proverbs 8:10
Psalm 37:16	1 Timothy 6:10
Proverbs 11:4	Psalm 62:10
Mark 10:24	Romans 2:4
Ephesians 3:8	1 Timothy 6:17
Proverbs 10:2	Psalm 19:10
Matthew 6:19-20	1 Peter 1:7
Proverbs 23:5	Proverbs 22:1
Psalm 119:14	Romans 6:23
Proverbs 11:28	Psalm 119:127

Discussion
Which is better — to be a millionaire without Jesus or to be poor and have Jesus as your Savior? Can money buy you happiness? Can it buy you a home in heaven? Which is better — to give or to receive? If you had to choose between having thousands of gold and silver coins or the Bible, which would you choose?

7. Name The Time Of Day

Materials Needed

A cardboard clock with a red hand and a blue hand, a felt marker, a brass paper fastener, masking tape

Preparation

Make a large cardboard clock and mark the numbers 1 to 12 on it. Attach a red and a blue cardboard hand to the clock with a brass paper fastener. Cover the prongs on the back with tape.

How to Play

1. Divide the players into two teams, the red and the blue. Place both hands of the clock at twelve. Conduct a Bible drill, using the verses about time. The first player to step forward must read the verse and tell what time of day is mentioned. (Some verses mention more than one.)

2. If the player reads the correct verse and states the right time of day, move his team's hand forward one number. If he reads an incorrect verse or gets the time of day wrong, move the hand back one number. In that case, the next player who stepped forward may try to earn the point.

3. The team whose hand first goes all around the clock and back to 12 is the winner.

Alternate Suggestion

The clock may be used for a quiz on Bible times of day or for other quizzes or Bible drills.

What Is The Time Of Day?
Genesis 1:5 (morning and evening)
1 Samuel 20:35 (evening)
Exodus 40:38 (day and night)
Genesis 19:27 (morning)
Psalm 119:62 (midnight)
John 1:39 (the tenth hour — about 4 p.m. our time)
Genesis 28:18 (morning)
Matthew 14:23 (evening)
Exodus 16:13 (morning and evening)
Acts 5:19 (night)
Psalm 1:2 (day and night)
2 Chronicles 7:12 (night)
Lamentations 3:23 (morning)
Acts 22:6 (noon)
Luke 2:8 (night)
Acts 16:25 (midnight)
Joshua 6:12 (morning)
Psalm 55:17 (evening, morning, noon)

1. Mountain Climbers And Giant Killers

Before playing this game the first time, tell the story of Caleb, who claimed the mountain which God had given him, even though giants lived there. He climbed the mountain, fought the giants, and lived on his mountain. (*See Joshua 12:6-15; 13:13.*)

We have a mountain to climb — the "mountain" of doing God's will. The "giants" are fear and discouragement. Maybe we are afraid others will make fun of us for obeying God. Or maybe we fail to do right, because we forget to trust God to help us. Let this game remind you to trust God and fight those giants of fear and discouragement.

Materials Needed

Cardboard file folders, scissors, glue, forty index cards, a 5x5-inch square of cardboard, a paper clip, a paper fastener, and game markers (buttons or pennies, one per player)

Preparation

Duplicate a game sheet and playing instructions for each player and two sheets of the cards. Glue or staple each game sheet to the inside of a file folder on the right. Glue the instructions on the left. Cut apart the cards and glue each one to an index card. To make the spinner, duplicate the pattern, cut it out, and glue it to the square of cardboard. Attach a paper clip spinner in the center with a paper fastener. Tape the prongs to the back of the card.

Spinner Pattern

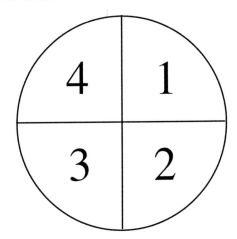

Playing Instructions

The object of the game is to see which player can reach the top of the mountain first. Place all the playing cards in the center of the players, face down. Each player puts his marker at the bottom of the mountain.

Taking turns, the players spin the spinner and move their marker the number of spaces indicated. If a player lands on a space occupied by a giant, he must draw a card from the pile and follow the instructions. If all the cards are used before the game ends, shuffle them and make a new pile.

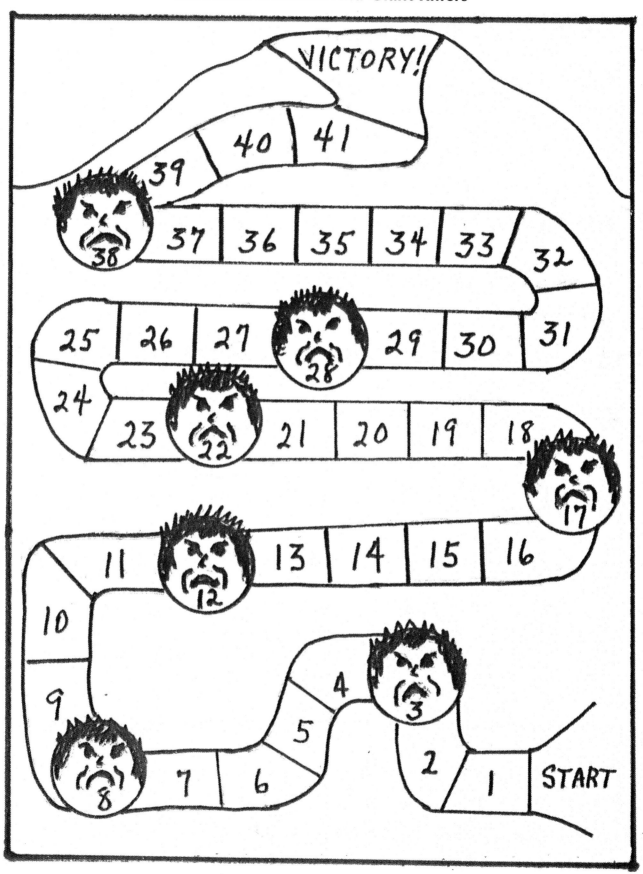

Playing Cards

You trust the Lord and are not afraid. Go ahead 1 space.	You trust the Lord and are not afraid. Take another turn.
You trust the Lord and are not afraid. Go ahead 2 spaces.	You trust the Lord and are not afraid. Take another turn.
You trust the Lord and are not afraid. Go ahead 3 spaces.	You trust the Lord and are not afraid. Take another turn.
You trust the Lord and are not afraid. Go ahead 1 space.	You trust the Lord and are not afraid. Take 2 extra turns.
You trust the Lord and are not afraid. Go ahead 2 spaces.	You trust the Lord and are not afraid. Take 2 extra turns.
You are afraid and discouraged. Go back 3 spaces.	You are afraid and discouraged. Lose 1 turn.
You are afraid and discouraged. Go back 2 spaces.	You are afraid and discouraged. Lose 1 turn.
You are afraid and discouraged. Go back 1 space.	You are afraid and discouraged. Lose 1 turn.
You are afraid and discouraged. Go back 2 spaces.	You are afraid and discouraged. Lose 2 turns.
You are afraid and discouraged. Go back 1 space.	You are afraid and discouraged. Lose 2 turns.

2. The Growing Game

Purpose

To help pupils learn what activities will help them grow as Christians and which will hinder their growth

Materials Needed

Cardboard file folders, crayons or felt pens, construction paper, paper clips, paper fasteners, transparent tape

Preparation

1. Prepare as many games as needed for every two to four players, following these directions for each: Duplicate the game pattern, tokens, and directions. Glue the game, number wheel, and directions to a file folder. With felt pens or crayons, color a frame around the squares which have words on the game pattern as follows: BIBLE — blue, PRAYER — yellow, CHURCH — green, PARENTS AND TEACHERS — red, MET SINNER — purple, SINNED — black.

2. Duplicate four copies of the word cards for each game. Cut them apart and glue them to 3x4-inch pieces of construction paper, using the same colors as above. Cut apart the tokens and glue them to cardboard. If you wish, laminate or cover everything with clear Con-tact paper for preservation.

3. Use the spinner from the previous game or make another by the same directions.

Discussion

Before playing the game the first time, explain to the pupils that Jesus is their perfect pattern for growth. As they make it their goal to become more like him, they will be steadily growing as Christians.

The squares on the game board tell of times in their lives when they must decide what to do. If they do right, they will grow. If they do wrong, they won't grow. Explain any wording on the cards which your pupils don't understand. Read 2 Peter 3:18.

Playing Directions (*glue to the file folder*)

(*For two to four players*) Place the word cards, face down, in the middle of the table in piles according to their colors. Taking turns, spin the spinner and move your token the same number of spaces the spinner stops on. If you land on a square with a colored frame, draw one card of that color from the pile. Move forward or go back, as the card tells you to do. See who can reach the goal first. Best of all, learn what will help you grow more like Jesus and what will keep you from growing.

Playing Cards

BIBLE You read it every day. Move ahead 2 spaces.	**BIBLE** You forgot to read it. Go back 2 spaces.
PRAYER You pray every day. Move ahead 1 space.	**PRAYER** You forgot to pray. Go back 1 space.
CHURCH You went last Sunday. Move ahead 2 spaces.	**CHURCH** You stayed away last Sunday. Go back 2 spaces.
PARENTS AND TEACHERS You obeyed. Move ahead 2 spaces.	**PARENTS AND TEACHERS** You disobeyed. Go back 2 spaces.
MET SINNER You witnessed for Jesus. Move ahead 1 space.	**MET SINNER** You didn't witness for Jesus. Go back 1 space.
SINNED You asked God to forgive you. Move ahead 3 spaces.	**SINNED** You didn't ask God to forgive. Go back 3 spaces.

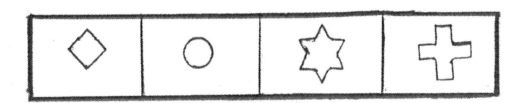

Tokens

The Growing Game

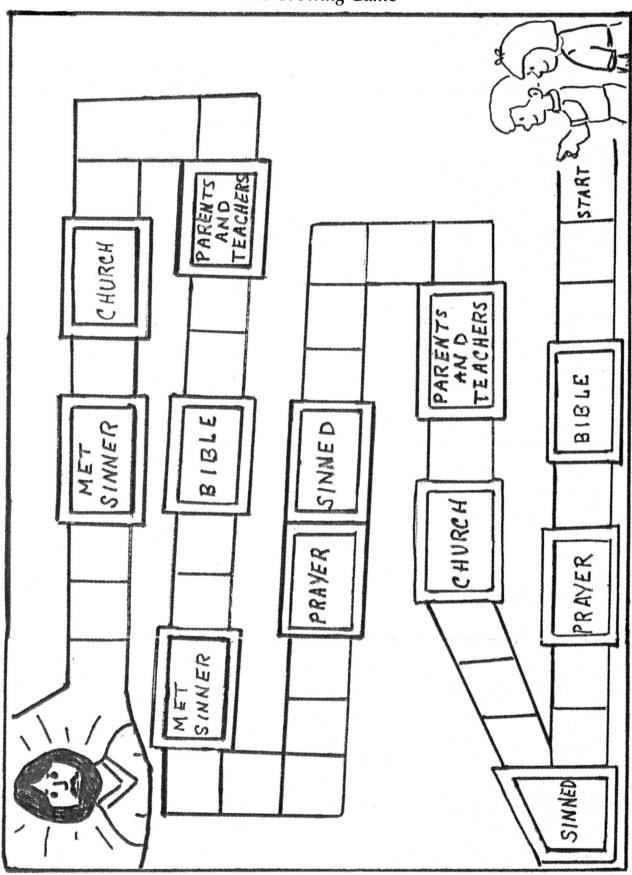

1. Good Guys And Bad Guys

Materials Needed

A felt pen and 23 index cards

Preparation

Print each Bible character's name, listed below, on a separate card. In a corner of the card, print GG (Good Guys) or BG (Bad Guys).

How to Play

1. Divide the players into two teams of equal numbers. If you have an extra player, he will be the "escort" (described later). Assign one team to be the Bad Guys and the other team to be the Good Guys. Give each player a card to hold, good or bad, according to his team. Explain that all the cards have names of Bible characters. The bad guys committed a crime or did something else bad. The good guys, while not perfect, loved God and tried to obey Him.

2. The teams stand in two lines, facing each other. Designate one place in your room as the prison and another place as the the bad guys' hideout. If there is an extra player, he will escort bad guys to the prison and good guys to the hideout.

3. Have all the players hold their name cards in front of them. Name a clue about any bad guy to the first good guy. He tries to name the bad guy it describes. If he is right, that bad guy is escorted to prison. If he is wrong, say so, but don't reveal who the correct character is. Continue, until all the good guys have received a clue.

4. Name a clue to each bad guy, including those in prison. When they identify a good guy, he is escorted to the bad guys' hideout.

5. Continue in the same manner, repeating the clues, until all members of each team have had three turns. The team with the most members still in line is the winner. When you play the game again, you may want to give each team only two turns.

The Bad Guys' Clues

Cain	I was the first murderer, and I killed my own brother.
Pharaoh	I made the Israelites be my slaves and would not let them leave. Then God sent me ten plagues.
Achan	I fought in the battle of Jericho and took gold, silver, and a garment, against God's orders.
Goliath	I was a huge Philistine soldier who challenged any Israelite soldier to come out and fight me.
King Saul	I was the first king of Israel, but I lost my throne because I disobeyed God.
Absalom	I led a rebellion against my father, the king, and I caught my long hair in a tree and died.
Jezebel	I was a wicked queen who was thrown out of a window, and my body was eaten by dogs.
King Nebuchadnezzar	I threw three men in a fiery furnace because they would not bow down to my golden image.
King Belshazzar	I drank wine from the cups out of God's temple, and I saw a hand writing on my wall.
Herod	I tried to kill Baby Jesus by killing all the babies who were two years old or younger.
Judas Iscariot	I betrayed Jesus to his enemies, who killed him on the cross.

The Good Guys' Clues

Noah	I built a boat that floated above the mountains.
Abraham	I had a son when I was 100 years old, and I became the father of the Israelite nation.
Joseph	I was sold as a slave in Egypt and became the ruler next to Pharaoh.
Moses	I led the children of Israel through the wilderness and to the border of Canaan.
Samuel	When I was a little boy, my mother gave me to God to serve in the temple.
David	I killed a lion, a bear, and a giant, and I became the king of Israel.
Elijah	I did not die, but I went up to heaven in a whirlwind, with a chariot of fire.
Daniel	I prayed three times a day by my window, and so I was thrown into the lions' den.
Peter	I walked on the water like Jesus.
John	My brother James and I were fishermen who left our nets to follow Jesus.
Stephen	I was the first person to be killed for being a Christian.
Paul	I persecuted Christians. Then I believed in Jesus and was a missionary to the Gentiles.

2. Secret Chair

Materials Needed

Chairs, masking tape, a felt marker, a piano or a cassette player with a music tape

Preparation

To the back of each chair (one per pupil), stick a small piece of masking tape and write a number on it. (Starting with #1, write consecutive numbers.) Place the chairs in a large circle, facing inward.

How to Play

1. The players stand inside the circle. As music is played, they march around until the music stops. Then they sit on the nearest chair. (If you have no music say "Go" and "Stop.")

2. Using the following list or one of your own choosing, state the number that is the secret chair. The players look on the back of their chairs to see what their number is. The one who is sitting in the secret chair identifies himself.

3. In order to remain in the game, he must do the stated requirement for that number. If he fails to do it, he must drop out of the game. Do not remove a chair.

4. Continue as above, until you call time or only one player remains. Those still in the game are the winners.

Secret Chair Numbers and Requirements

Numbers 1-15 are given. If you have more than fifteen players, add your own requirements to the list. If you have less than fifteen, use the extra requirements with any smaller numbers. After using all of the list, go back and repeat it, if necessary. End the game at any time.

 1. Number 5:   Name five books of the Old Testament.
 2. Number 2:   Name five books of the New Testament.
 3. Number 10: Crow like the rooster that Peter heard when he denied Jesus.
 4. Number 1:   Name five disciples of Jesus.
 5. Number 11: Walk like an elephant going into Noah's ark.
 6. Number 12: Name two Bible towns.
 7. Number 6:   March around our circle and "blow" a ram's horn, like a priest going around Jericho.
 8. Number 4:   Name two of the Ten Commandments.
 9. Number 8:   Name four men in the Bible.
10. Number 15: Hop like the frogs in the Egyptian plague.
11. Number 3:   Name four women in the Bible.
12. Number 9:   Name the first and last books of the Bible.
13. Number 13: Make the animal noise of the beast that talked to Balaam.
14. Number 7:   Name five animals that God created.
15. Number 14: Make a sound like the animals that the Prodigal Son fed.

3. Going To Church Tag

How to Play

1. Teach or review Psalm 122:1 before playing this game.

2. Choose one child to be "IT." Place all the other players at one end of the room or playground and mark a parallel goal line as far away as possible. This is the "church."

3. Ring a bell or say, "Time for church," which is a signal for the players to run toward the church. "IT" tags as many as possible. The tagged players then help "IT" catch others. The game continues until all players have either reached the church or are in the center. The ones who reached the church are the winners.

4. Say, "Someone doesn't want you to go to church. Who is he?" (*Satan.*) What are some excuses he puts in your mind for not going to church? (*Some suggestions: "You're too tired. You want to watch TV. It's more fun to play outside."*) Encourage your pupils to attend church gladly and faithfully.

4. Walls, Fall Down

Purpose

To review the story of the conquest of Jericho and to help pupils learn the names of the twelve tribes of Israel

Preparation

On a slip of paper, copy the names of the twelve tribes of Israel to use as the game is played. (See the list below. Ephraim and Manasseh, named for Joseph's two sons, were half tribes, so they are called together.) Before playing the game the first time, review the story in Joshua 6 of the fall of Jericho. In the game, the children will pretend to be the Israelites, marching around the walls of Jericho.

How to Play

1. Make a large ring of chairs, facing outward. There will be one less chair than players. This represents the walls of Jericho. Give each player the name of a tribe of Israel. If you have more than twelve players, give the same name to two or more players. An adult leader plays the part of Joshua, who calls out the names of the tribes.

2. As Joshua calls the names of the tribes, the children who have those names get up and follow the leader around the circle. At any time, Joshua may call out, "Walls, fall down." All marchers try to sit down, and the one without a chair drops out of the game. Remove one chair and continue the game until only one player is left. This is the winner.

3. As players become familiar with the names of the tribes, let one of them try to take the part of Joshua.

The Twelve Tribes Of Israel

Reuben	Zebulun	Asher
Simeon	Issachar	Naphtali
Levi	Dan	Ephraim-Manasseh
Judah	Gad	Benjamin

5. Seven Ducks In Muddy Water

Purpose

To review the story of Naaman's cleansing from leprosy and to teach that obeying God is better than choosing our own way

Materials Needed

Two beanbags, balls, or similar objects

Preparation

(*Tell the story of Naaman from 2 Kings 5 and read verse 10.*) These words of Elisha to Naaman were really a command of God. Naaman didn't want to wash in the Jordan River, because it was muddy. How many times was he supposed to go under the muddy water? Seven! That's seven ducks in muddy water, isn't it? At last, Naaman obeyed God and ducked under the water seven times. At once, he was healed! If we want God's blessings, we must obey His commands, even if don't like to do them or understand why He gives them.

How to Play

1. Divide the players into two teams and choose team captains. Seat each team in a circle, facing inward. Place a beanbag or other small object at the feet of each captain.

2. At a signal, each captain picks up his beanbag and passes it to the player on his right. It goes around the circle until it returns to the captain. He calls out loudly, "One duck in muddy water!" Continue to pass the beanbag and count its times around until one captain wins by calling out, "Seven ducks in muddy water!" (*Monitor the calls to be sure a captain counts correctly.*) If a beanbag is dropped, it must be returned to the captain to begin that round again.

3. The team which finishes first gets ten points. Play as many times as you wish, but end with an even number of games. The team with the highest score wins.

6. March To Canaan

Purpose

To review the story of Israel's journey from Egypt to Canaan and to show that we, too, should obey God's commands

Preparation

You will need a large playing area, either inside or outside, because this game is similar to "Red Light." Designate one end of the area as Egypt. The other end — the finish line — is Canaan. In between is the wilderness. The players are the Israelites. The leader represents God.

Discussion

(*To do before playing the game the first time.*) On the Israelites' journey to Canaan from Egypt, how did God show them that He was present with them? (*By a cloud in the daytime and a pillar of fire at night.*) When the cloud or pillar of fire moved ahead, they knew they should march. When it stopped, they stopped. When they reached the border of Canaan, though, the adult Israelites refused to go in, because they were afraid of the giants in the land. Instead of going into Canaan, they had to wander in the wilderness for forty years. Then their children went into Canaan and lived in the land. It always pays to obey God, doesn't it?

How to Play

1. All players line up along the starting line (Egypt). When the leader calls, "March," they begin marching. When the leader calls, "Stop," all must stop in place and freeze. If anyone moves, he must go back to the beginning of the wilderness, standing just in front of the starting line, and begin his march again.

2. The first five who reach the finish line (Canaan) are the winners. All others are the Israelites who died in the wilderness, because they did not obey God.

7. Hold On!

Purpose

To demonstrate to children that they should pay attention and learn when they hear or read the Bible and when it is taught to them

Materials Needed

A rubber ball

Discussion

(*Read Proverbs 4:13.*) What should we hold on to and not let it go? (*Instruction.*) This is talking about the teachings of the Bible. It tells us how God wants us to live. How do you suppose you can "hold on to" the teachings of the Bible? (*By listening to it carefully, trying to understand it, and obeying it.*)

The devil doesn't want you to hold on to God's teachings. He may tempt you to whisper or write notes in class during the Bible teaching. Let's play a game to remind you to hold on to the teachings of the Bible and not let the devil take them away from you.

How to Play

1. Choose one player to be "IT." All the other players stand in a circle around "IT," with their feet wide apart and touching those of the player on either side. "IT" tries to roll the ball outside the circle, going between a player's feet. The players must not move their feet but may try to stop the ball with their hands. If "IT" succeeds in rolling the ball out of the circle, the player who let the ball escape is the next "IT."

8. Capture A Prisoner

Purpose

Playing this game will help children learn the names of Bible characters or books.

How to Play

1. Choose a person to be "IT." Divide the remaining players into two teams and line them up on two opposite sides of a room or other playing area.

2. Choose a category of Bible characters (tribes of Israel, prophets, disciples, men, women, children, and so on) or Bible books (Law, History, Poetry, Major Prophets, and so on). Tell the children what the category is. Beginning at one end of a line, give each member of one team a different name in the category. Repeat the same names for the other team, but reverse the order, like this:

    Team One: Adam, Noah, Abraham, Isaac, Jacob, Joseph, Joshua

    Team Two: Joshua, Joseph, Jacob, Isaac, Abraham, Noah, Adam

3. "IT" stands between the two lines. An adult leader calls out one of the names. The two children who have that name try to exchange places, with "IT" attempting to catch one or both of them as his prisoners.

4. Choose a spot on the sidelines to be the prison, where captured prisoners must go. Continue playing, with "IT" catching all he can. If there is only one person left with a certain name, he runs across to the opposite line alone when his name is called and tries to avoid being caught.

5. The game is over when there are no more players left in line. The first person who was caught becomes the next "IT." The names of characters or books from other categories may be used each time you play, if you wish.

9. People And Places

Purpose
To help pupils learn to associate Bible characters to places which were important in their lives

Materials Needed
Small cards, one per pupil; masking tape; a felt marker

Preparation
On half the cards or slips of paper, print the names of Bible characters from the list below. On the other half, print the places listed. Center a piece of masking tape at the top of each card, leaving an end above the card for taping to a player's chest. Tell the pupils that each of the Bible characters whose name is on a card can be matched with a place that was very important in his life. They will be hunting for the person or place that matches their card.

How to Play
1. Choose one or more adult referees to judge if the players have made the right match. Tell the players who these are.

2. Give each player a game card, blank side up. The players must not turn their cards over until a signal is given. Then each player looks at the name of the person or place on his card, tapes his card to his chest, and begins to move about, trying to find the matching card.

3. As soon as two players think their cards match, they come to a referee for a confirmation. If the person and place match, they may be seated. If not, they must continue to search.

4. The first two players to finish receive a score of ten points each. Give five points each for finishing second and two points each for finishing third.

5. When all cards have been matched, collect them, mix them up, and give them out to play again, several times. The player with the highest total score wins.

Another Way to Play
1. For a small class, do not put tape on the cards. Put all the place cards, face down, in a bag or box. Give each player a card with a person's name. Then he takes one card from the bag or box.

2. At a signal, the players turn over their place cards. If they think they have a match, they check with a referee at once. If not, they move around, looking at each other's cards and trying to find the place card that matches their person card. When a player finds his matching card, he exchanges his place card for it. Then proceed as in the previous instructions.

List Of Bible People And Places

Adam	Garden of Eden
Noah	Ark
Abraham	Ur
Lot	Sodom and Gomorrah
Joseph	Egypt (prison; palace)
Moses	Red Sea
Aaron	Tabernacle (Most Holy Place)
Joshua	Jericho
Elijah	Mt. Carmel
David	Facing Goliath
Jonah	Whale's stomach
Daniel	Lions' den
Shadrach, Meshach, Abednego	Fiery furnace
Baby Jesus	Manger in Bethlehem
Peter and Andrew	Sea of Galilee
Mary (Martha's sister)	At feet of Jesus
Jesus (Man)	On the cross
John the Baptist	Jordan River
Zacchaeus	Sycamore tree
Saul (Paul)	Road to Damascus
John, the disciple	Isle of Patmos

10. The Lord Is My Shepherd

Purpose

To think about Jesus as our Shepherd — the one who watches over us and takes care of us

Materials Needed

Four photocopies of the game pattern, a paper bag, construction paper, glue, scissors

Preparation

Glue two game patterns to sheets of construction paper of one color and two sheets to paper of another color. (Be sure to cover the entire pattern with glue.) Cut apart the letters and pictures of one sheet of each color. The remaining two sheets are game boards. Place all the letters and pictures, mixed together, in a medium-sized bag. Before playing the game the first time, have the following discussion:

Discussion

Do you know what a shepherd used his rod and staff for? (*To lead the sheep to green grass or water and to pull them back to safety when they wandered away. He also used them to protect the sheep from a wolf or other wild animal.*) Why do you think he poured oil on the heads of his sheep? (*To heal scratches and sores, and so forth.*) Jesus said that he is our Shepherd. Just as a shepherd cares for his sheep, Jesus will take care of us and help us to have what we need.

How to Play

1. Seat the players around a table or in a circle on the floor. Divide the players into two teams by counting one-two around the circle, so that every other player is on the same team. If the two teams are not equal in number, an adult helper can play on one team. Choose a captain for each team and give him a game board. Each captain will place his team's letters and pictures on its game board.

2. Let the captains draw straws to see which team will begin first. Give the paper bag to the captain with the long straw. He draws out one playing piece from the paper bag.

3. If it has his team's color, he places it on its match on his team's game board and passes the bag to the player on his right. If the piece he draws is not in his team's color, he puts it back in the bag, mixes up the playing pieces, and passes the bag to the next player. Continue, with each player giving his captain the playing piece he draws out, if it has his team's color.

4. If a player draws out a picture in his team's color, it is placed on the game board, but then the rules are different. For drawing out the rod and staff, the grass and water, or the horn of oil, the player gets an extra turn. If he draws out a wolf, two letters from his team's board must be placed back in the bag. The team which first completes everything on its game board is the winner.

5. If the class is large, make four sets of the game and play two games simultaneously. In a class of five or less, make a game set for each player and let each one play for himself.

THE / LORD IS MY SHEPHERD

Index

Angels

Bible Characters And Animals

Bible Facts

Bible Stories

God: Jesus

Memory Work

Salvation And Christian Living